Japanese Reader Collection Volume 7: The Little Match Girl

The Easy Way to Read, Listen, and Learn from Japanese Folklore, Tales, and Stories

Clay & Yumi Boutwell

Cover art based on Helen Stratton's 1899 Illustration for <u>The Fairy Tales of Hans Christian Andersen</u>

English version based on the 1913 translation by H.L. Brækstad

Copyright © 2017 Kotoba Books
www.ClayBoutwell.com
www.TheJapanShop.com

All rights reserved.

ISBN: 1544011873
ISBN-13: 978-1544011875

YOU ARE NOT ALONE IN YOUR JAPANESE LANGUAGE JOURNEY!

JOIN OUR NEW FACEBOOK GROUP

We have a **brand new Facebook group** specifically for our readers.

Get answers to your questions while going through this or any of our books, post your question in the group! If you spot errors or inconsistencies, please post that too. Have requests for future volumes? We'd love to hear from you.

Find us on

https://www.facebook.com/groups/1875878879339553/
Or do a search in Facebook for the group called:
"Learn Japanese: Clay & Yumi"

This group is for discussing any of Clay & Yumi's books on learning Japanese. It may be quiet as this is a new group, but don't be shy! If you have any question about Japanese or about anything found in this book (errors, questions, suggestions), please post.

INTRODUCTION

The key to learning vocabulary is, quite simply, reading. Not only are you more likely to pick up words that interest you, but you also learn them **in context**. The **Japanese Reader Collection Series** goes one step further by adding **MP3s of the Japanese**. Improve your **listening comprehension** while building your **vocabulary, kanji,** and **reading skills**.

FORMAT OF THIS READER

By choosing **short stories**, the intimidation factor is greatly reduced. Not only that, but we divide the story up into tiny, easy-to-swallow segments with complete explanations to give you confidence as you read **real Japanese** page by page.

The stories are selected to represent certain key aspects of Japanese culture. The tales, characters, and even moral lessons are often found in Japanese conversation, movies, and manga. Knowing these stories in this series will go well beyond simply improving your language skills. **It will help you understand Japanese culture as well.**

WHO IS THIS FOR?

This book is designed so that both those fairly new to Japanese and those in the intermediate stages can equally get value out of it. We recommend learning hiragana first, but we are also including rōmaji in the definitions so you can be sure you are reading with the correct pronunciation. For a quick two-week crash course for mastering hiragana, please see our book: Hiragana, the Basics of Japanese.

FEATURES

- **Line-by-line:** Read the story broken down line-by-line with nearly every vocabulary word defined and explained.
- **Grammatical Notes:** In this section, we go through important grammatical patterns found in the story and attempt to explain them in plain English. The grammar icon 文法 found in the line-by-line definitions indicates there is a note for that word or phrase.
- **Full Japanese with Furigana:** Read the full story in *real* Japanese. Every kanji has furigana above

it. Furigana is the small hiragana above kanji so even beginners can work through the text.

  • **English Version:** Lastly, we are including a simple English translation. This should be avoided until you are sure you understand the story or find it too difficult to figure out on your own.

You may want to try to read the story in Japanese with furigana while listening to the MP3s first. Or if you are a beginner, it may be better to go through the line-by-line story before attempting the full Japanese text. Any way you do it, **this book offers several ways to read, listen, and learn.**

- **Kanji in Focus:** This is a new section to help with the incredibly difficult task of learning those pesky Chinese characters. We take many of the kanji found in the story and present the readings, meaning(s), and give an example sentence:

READINGS	ヤ; よ; よる
MEANING	night; evening
EXAMPLE	夜中(よなか) midnight; middle of the night

- **MP3s:** Included at no extra charge are two MP3s of the story. One is read at the normal speed and the other at a slow, easy-to-follow pace. If the MP3s were not included when you purchased this book, please see the last page for a download link. If you have ANY trouble downloading, please email us at help@thejapanshop.com.

v

ABOUT The Little Match Girl

The famous Hans Christian Andersen short story has found its way into Japanese culture being a well-known tale in Japan. The sad story is about a dying little girl's dreams and desires on a cold New Year's Eve. It was first published in 1845 in Danish.

ABOUT CLAY & YUMI

Yumi was a popular radio DJ in Japan for over ten years. She has extensive training in standard Japanese pronunciation which makes her perfect for creating these language instructional audio files.

Clay has been a passionate learner of Japanese for over twenty years now. His free language learning website, www.TheJapanesePage.com, got its start back in 1999 as a way to help other learners of Japanese as well as himself.

In 2002, they opened www.TheJapanShop.com to help students of Japanese get hard-to-find Japanese books.

Yumi and I are **very grateful** for your purchase and we truly hope this book will help you improve your Japanese. **We love our customers and don't take a single one of you for granted.** If you have any questions about this book or Japanese in general, I invite you to contact me below by email or on social media.

Clay & Yumi Boutwell (and Makoto & Megumi)
clay@thejapanshop.com

@theJapanShop | @ClayBoutwell
www.facebook.com/JapaneseReader

http://www.TheJapanShop.com
http://www.TheJapanesePage.com
http://www.ClayBoutwell.com

P.S. Please see the last page of the book to find the download link for the MP3s of these stories free of charge.

CONTENTS

Table of Contents

INTRODUCTION	iii
WANT A FREE BOOK (or three)?	10
The Little Match Girl with Running Gloss	11
The Little Match Girl Grammatical Notes	46
The Little Match-Seller in Japanese	54
The Little Match Girl English Summary	71
Kanji in Focus	75
VOCABULARY	79
DOWNLOAD LINK	105
Also by Clay & Yumi Boutwell	106

マッチ<ruby>売<rt>う</rt></ruby>りの<ruby>少女<rt>しょうじょ</rt></ruby>

The Little Match Seller by Hans Christian Andersen

 This tragic story is popular in Japanese culture—moreso, I think, than in the US—and is often referenced in Japanese culture. For example, the kindergarten-aged manga hero, Crayon Shinchan often dons a head scarf and plays the role of the little match seller for sympathy and comic effect.

www.TheJapanShop.com

WANT A FREE BOOK (or three)?

Get your copy of **Kanji 100 absolutely free** today.

That includes the Kindle, ePub, PDF versions. We'll even included all the MP3s for all the examples found in the book.

Simply go to http://www.TheJapanShop.com and click on **"GET MY FREE BOOK"** today!

AND!

If you like fiction, get two of Clay's books FREE. Check out his author site and click on **"Yes, send me my books"**: http://ClayBoutwell.com/

The Little Match Girl with Running Gloss

マッチ売りの少女

とても寒い日のことでした。雪も降っていて、もうあたりはすっかり暗くなっていて、それは今年さいごの夜のことでした。

とても寒い *totemo samui*—very cold
とても寒い日のことでした *totemo samui hi no koto deshita*—it happened on a very cold day 文法
雪も *yuki mo*—snow also (was falling)
降っていて *futte ite*—falling (snowing) 文法
もう *mō*—already
あたり *atari*—the area; nearby
すっかり *sukkari*—completely; thoroughly
暗くなっていて *kuraku natte ite*—it became completely dark
それは *sore wa*—as for that
今年 *kotoshi*—this year
さいご *saigo*—last; final
夜 *yoru*—night
今年さいごの夜のことでした *kotoshi saigo no yoru no koto deshita*—It was the last night of the year

その寒さと暗闇の中、一人のかわいそうな女の子が道を歩いていました。

頭に何もかぶらず、裸足でした。

その寒さ *sono samusa*—that degree of coldness 文法
と *to*—and
暗闇 *kurayami*—darkness
〜の中 *~no naka*—in the midst (of the cold and darkness) 文法
一人 *hitori*—one person
かわいそうな *kawai sō na*—pitiful (girl)
女の子 *onna no ko*—girl
道 *michi*—road; street
歩いていました *aruite imashita*—had walked 文法
頭に *atama ni*—on (her) head (the に indicates location)
何も *nani mo*—nothing (on her head) [followed by a negative verb]
かぶらず *kaburazu*—didn't wear 文法
裸足 *hadashi*—barefoot

家を出るときには確かに靴をはいていました。

でも、靴は何の役にも立ちませんでした。それは大きすぎたのです。昔、女の子のお母さんがはいていたものでした。

家 ie—house
出るときに deru toki ni—at the time of leaving 文法
確かに tashika ni—certainly; surely
靴 kutsu—shoe
はいていました haite imashita—was wearing (shoes)
でも demo—but; however
何の nan no—what kind; what sort
役にも立ちませんでした yaku ni mo tachimasen deshita—not at all useful 文法
それは sore wa—that is; as for that...
大きすぎた ooki sugita—was too big 文法
のです no desu—[sentence ender for explanations]
昔 mukashi—a long time ago
女の子 onna no ko—girl
お母さん okaasan—mother
もの mono—[used to express emotional involvement]

女の子が道を渡ろうとした時、二台の馬車がすごい速さで走ってきたので、彼女は靴を無くしてしまったのです。

片方の靴はどこにも見つかりません

道 *michi*—road; street
を *o*—[direct object marker]
渡ろうとした *watarō to shita*—intended to cross (the street) 文法
時 *toki*—the time (she tried to cross the street)
二台 *ni dai*—two (carriages) 文法
馬車 *basha*—horse drawn carriage; coach 文法
すごい速さ *sugoi hayasa*—very fast; extreme speed
走ってきた *hashitte kita*—running [the きた is used to show becoming, coming to be, growing]
彼女 *kanojo*—she
靴 *kutsu*—shoes
無くしてしまった *naku shite shimatta*—unfortunately lost (her shoes) 文法
のです *no desu*—[sentence ender showing explanation or emphasis] 文法
片方 *katahō*—one side (one shoe)
どこにも *doko ni mo*—nowhere [use with negative verb]
見つかりません *mitsukarimasen*—cannot be found

でした。もう片方は、男の子が持っていってしまいました。自分に子供ができたら、ゆりかごにするんだと言って。

それで女の子は小さな裸の足で歩いていきました。

もう片方 *mō katahō*—the other side (shoe) 文法
男の子 *otoko no ko*—boy
持っていって *motte itte*—to take; carry (something) away
しまいました *shimaimashita*—[shows completion often with regret]
自分に *jibun ni*—to himself (have children himself)
子供 *kodomo*—children
できたら *dekitara*—if (he has children)
ゆりかご *yurikago*—cradle
にする *ni suru*—to make (shoe) into (cradle)
んだ *n da*—the expectation is that... [sentence ender when explaining]
言って *itte*—saying
それで *sore de*—and; thereupon; because of that
女の子 *onna no ko*—girl
小さな *chiisa na*—small (barefoot)
裸のあし *hadaka no ashi*—barefoot (lit. naked feet)

両足は冷たさのために赤く、また青くなっていました。

女の子は、古いエプロンの中にたくさんのマッチを入れていて、手にその一たばを持っていました。

両足 *ryō ashi*—both feet 文法
冷たさ *tsumetasa*—coldness; degree of cold
のために *no tame ni*—because of (the cold)
赤く *akaku*—(turned) red
また *mata*—and; also
青く *aoku*—(turned) blue
なっていました *natte imashita*—turned (blue); becoming
古い *furui*—old
エプロン *epuron*—apron
の中に *no naka ni*—inside; in the midst (of the apron)
たくさん *takusan*—many
マッチ *macchi*—matches
入れていて *irete ite*—were put; placed (inside)
手に *te ni*—in hand
その一たば *sono hito taba*—that single bundle 文法
持っていました *motte imashita*—carried

その日一日、誰も女の子から何も買ってくれませんでした。

一円だってくれる人はいなかったのです。

寒さと空腹で震えながら、女の子は歩き回りました。かわいそうな

その日 *sono hi*—that day
一日 *ichi nichi*—all day
誰も *dare mo*—no one
女の子から *onna no ko kara*—from the girl
何も *nani mo*—nothing 文法
買ってくれません *katte kuremasen*—wouldn't buy
一円 *ichi en*—one yen
だって *datte*—even
くれる *kureru*—receive (money)
人 *hito*—person
いなかった *inakatta*—weren't (any buyers)
のです *no desu*—[sentence ender showing explanation or emphasis]
寒さ *samusa*—degree of cold; coldness
空腹で *kuufuku de*—with hunger
震えながら *furue nagara*—while shaking 文法
歩き回りました *aruki mawarimashita*—walked around

子、まさに悲惨を絵に描いたようです。

雪が少女の長い金髪に舞い降りました。

その髪は首のまわりに美しくカールして下がっています。

かわいそうな子 *kawai sō na ko*—pitiful girl
まさに *masa ni*—certainly; truly
悲惨 *hisan*—tragedy; misery
絵 *e*—picture; painting
描いたよう *kaitayō*—as if drawn/painted
雪 *yuki*—snow
少女 *shōjo*—little girl
長い *nagai*—long
金髪 *kinpatsu*—golden hair; blonde
舞い降りました *mai orimashita*—swoop down upon (hair) 文法
その髪 *sono kami*—that hair
首 *kubi*—neck
まわりに *mawari ni*—around (the neck)
美しく *utsukushiku*—beautifully
カール *ka-ru*—curl
下がっています *sagatte imasu*—hang down (hair)

でも、もちろん、女の子は美しさのことなんか考えていません。

どの窓からも明かりが輝き、通りにはガチョウを焼いているおいしそうな香りがしました。

でも *demo*—but; however
もちろん *mochiron*—of course
美しさのこと *utsukushi sa no koto*—(her) beautifulness
なんか *nanka*—such a thing; or something like that... 文法
考えていません *kangaete imasen*—didn't think of
どの *dono*—every; any 文法
窓 *mado*—window
から *kara*—from
どの窓からも *dono mado kara mo*—from any window
明かり *akari*—light; illumination
輝き *kagayaki*—shined; radiated
通りには *toori ni wa*—and on the street
ガチョウ *gachō*—goose [kanji: 鵞鳥]
焼いている *yaite iru*—cooking; frying
おいしそう *oishi sō*—looks/smells delicious
香りがしました *kaori ga shimashita*—had a good scent

「今日は大晦日だわ。」女の子はそう思いました。

二つの家が街の角に並んで立っていました。

そのうち片方が前にせり出しています。

今日 *kyō*—today
大晦日 *oomisoka*—New Year's Eve 文法
わ *wa*—[feminine sentence ender] 文法
そう思いました *sō omoimashita*—thought like that
二つの *futatsu no*—two (houses)
家 *ie*—house
街の角に *machi no kado ni*—on a street corner
並んで *narande*—lined up
立っていました *tatte imashita*—standing; built
そのうち *sono uchi*—among these
片方 *katahō*—one side
前に *mae ni*—in front of
せり出しています *seri dashite imasu*—push out; to jut out; protrude

女の子はそこに座って小さくなりました。女の子は小さな足を体の下に引き寄せましたが、女の子はどんどん寒くなってきました。

けれど、家に帰るなんてできま

そこに soko ni—there
座って suwatte—sitting
小さくなりました chiisaku narimashita—became small
小さな足 chiisa na ashi—small legs 文法
体 karada—body
体の下に karada no shita ni—(pulled legs) under her body
引き寄せました hiki yosemashita—pulled toward oneself
が ga—but; however
どんどん don don—rapidly; steadily
寒くなってきました samuku natte kimashita—became cold
けれど keredo—but; however
家に帰る ie ni kaeru—to return home
なんて nante—such as; (things) like [used for emphasis of the absurdity of something]
できませんでした dekimasen deshite—couldn't (return home)

せんでした。

マッチは一本（いっぽん）も売（う）れていないし、たったの一円（いちえん）ももらえなかったのですから、このまま帰（かえ）ればお父（とう）さんに殴（なぐ）られてしまいます。

マッチ *macchi*—matches
一本も *ippon mo*—not even one (match) 文法
売れていない *urete inai*—didn't sell
し *shi*—[conjunction at the end of phrases that notes one of several reasons]
たったの *tatta no*—only; merely; but; no more than
一円も *ichien mo*—even one yen
もらえなかった *moraenakatta*—didn't receive
のです *no desu*—[ender showing explanation]
から *kara*—from
このまま *kono mama*—as is; without change
帰れば *kaereba*—if return (home) 文法
お父さん *otōsan*—father
に殴られてしまいます *ni nagurarete shimaimasu*—will be hit (by father)

それに家だって寒いのです。

頭の上に天井はありましたが、ビュービューと風が吹き込んでくるのです。わらとボロ布で塞いではありますが、大きなひびが入っているからです。

それに *sore ni*—besides; moreover
だって *datte*—after all; because
寒いのです *samui no desu*—it's cold 文法
頭の上に *atama no ue ni*—above (one's) head
天井 *tenjō*—ceiling
ありましたが *arimashita ga*—(ceiling) existed, but...
ビュービューと *byu- byu- to*—whistling (sound)
風 *kaze*—wind
吹き込んでくる *fuki konde kuru*—come blowing in 文法
わらと *wara to*—with straw
ボロぬの *boro nuno*—worn out cloth
塞いで *fusaide*—closed; blocked; shut up
ありますが *arimasu ga*—existed, but...
大きな *ooki na*—big
ひび *hibi*—crack
入っている *haitte iru*—entered; opened up (cracks)

女の子の小さな両手は冷たさのためにもう何も感じなくなっていました。

ああ！マッチがあるわ。たばの中からマッチを取り出して、壁にこすり付けて、火をつければ指を

小さな両手 *chiisa na ryōte*—both small hands
冷たさ *tsumeta sa*—coldness; the degree of cold
のために *no tame ni*—because of; due to...
もう *mō*—already
何も *nani mo*—nothing
感じなくなっていました *kanjinaku natte imashita*—lost feeling
ああ！ *aa!*—ah!
わ *wa*—[sentence ender used by women]
たばの中から *taba no naka kara*—from the bundle (of matches)
取り出して *tori dashite*—brought out
壁に *kabe ni*—to (on) the wall
こすり付けて *kosuri tsukete*—strike
火 *hi*—fire
つければ *tsukereba*—if lit (the match)
指 *yubi*—finger

温められるわ。

女の子は、マッチを一本取り出しました。シュッ！何という輝き。何とよく燃えることでしょう。

温かく、輝く炎で、上に手

温められる *atatamerareru*—be able to warm (fingers)
一本 *ippon*—one (match)
取り出しました *tori dashimashita*—brought out
シュッ！ *shuu!* [effect of striking a match]
何という *nan to iu*—how (bright)! 文法
輝き *kagayaki*—bright; radiant
何と *nan to*—how (well it burned)
よく燃えること *yoku moeru koto*—burning well
でしょう *deshō*—I think [used to express some certainty while still being polite]
温かく *atatakaku*—warming 文法
輝く *kagayaku*—shining; glittering
炎で *honoo de*—with a flame
上に *ue ni*—above
手 *te*—hand

をかざすとまるで小さなロウソクのようでした。

　すばらしい光です。女の子はまるで大きな鉄のストーブの前に座っているように思いました。

　そのストーブには光るしんちゅ

かざす *kazasu*—to hold up over one's head
まるで *marude*—as if; just like
小さな *chiisa na*—small
ロウソク *rōsoku*—candle
のようでした *no yō deshita*—as if (it were a candle) 文法
すばらしい光 *subarashii hikari*—wonderful light
大きな *ooki na*—big; large
鉄の *tetsu no*—an iron (stove)
ストーブ *suto-bu*—stove
の前に *no mae ni*—before; in front of
座っているように *suwatte iru yō ni*—as if sitting (in front of the stove)
思いました *omoimashita*—thought
そのストーブ *sono suto-bu*—that stove
光るしんちゅう *hikaru shinchuu*—shining brass
しんちゅうの足 *shinchuu no ashi*—brass legs (of the stove)

うの足があり、上にはしんちゅうの飾りがついていました。

なんと美しく燃える炎でしょう。

炎はまわりをあたためます。

女の子は足をのばして、あたたまろうとしました。

あり *ari*—have
上に *ue ni*—above
しんちゅうの飾り *shinchuu no kazari*—brass decorations
ついていました *tsuite imashita*—were attached
なんと美しく *nanto utsukushiku*—how beautifully (it burned)
燃える炎 *moeru honoo*—burning fire
まわり *mawari*—around
あたためます *atatamemasu*—to warm
足をのばして *ashi o nobashite*—stretch out (her) legs
あたたまろうとしました *atatamarō to shimashita*—intending to warm (her legs) 文法

しかし、——小さな炎は消え、ストーブも消えてしまいました。

手の中に燃え尽きたマッチだけが残っているだけでした。

女の子はもう一本壁にこすりました。マッチは明るく燃え、その

しかし shikashi—but; however
小さな炎 chiisa na honoo—a small flame
消え kie—extinguish
手の中に te no naka ni—in (her) hands
燃え尽きた moe tsukita—to burn out 文法
だけ dake—only
残っている nokotteiru—left over; remaining
もう一本 mō ippon—one more (match) 文法
こすりました kosurimashita—to rub; to strike
明るく燃え akaruku moe—burned brightly
その sono—that

明かりが壁にあたったところはヴェールのように透けて見えました。そして、女の子にはその向こうに部屋が見えました。

テーブルの上にはとても白いテーブルクロスが広げられ、その上

壁に *kabe ni*—on the wall
あたった *atatta*—hit; touched (where the light fell)
ところ *tokoro*—place
ヴェール *ve-ru*—veil
のように *no yō ni*—like; similar to (a veil)
透けて *sukete*—transparent
見えました *miemashita*—able to be seen
そして *soshite*—and then
向こうに *mukō ni*—other side; opposite side
部屋 *heya*—room
テーブルの上に *te-buru no ue ni*—on top of the table
とても *totemo*—very
白いテーブルクロス *shiroi te-buru kurosu*—white tablecloth
広げられ *hirogerare*—spread; extend; enlarge
その上に *sono ue ni*—on top of

には豪華な食器が並べられていました。

焼かれたガチョウにはりんごとプラムが詰められていて、おいしそうな湯気を上げていました。

そして、うれしいことに、ガチ

豪華 *gōka*—gorgeous; splendor 文法
食器 *shokki*—tableware
並べられていました *naraberarete imashita*—was lined up
焼かれた *yakareta*—cooked
ガチョウ *gachō*—goose [kanji: 鵞鳥]
りんご *ringo*—apple
プラム *puramu*—plum
詰められていて *tsumerarete ite*—stuffed into; jammed in
おいしそうな *oishi sō na*—delicious looking
湯気 *yuge*—steam; vapor
上げていました *agete imashita*—raised; elevated
そして *soshite*—and then
うれしいこと *ureshii koto*—a good thing; happily

ョウは、背中にナイフとフォークを刺したまま、テーブルから飛び降りて、よろよろと歩きながら、かわいそうな女の子のところまでやってきたのです。

と、その時、マッチは消えてし

背中に *senaka ni*—in the back
ナイフ *naifu*—knife
フォーク *fo-ku*—fork
刺したまま *sashita mama*—left stabbed (the knife) 文法
テーブル *te-buru*—table
から *kara*—from
飛び降りて *tobi orite*—jump down 文法
よろよろと *yoroyoro to*—tottering; unsteady on its feet
歩きながら *aruki nagara*—while walking
かわいそうな *kawai sō na*—pitiful
ところ *tokoro*—place
まで *made*—until
やってきた *yatte kita*—came along
のです *no desu*—[ender for explanations]
と *to*—and
その時 *sono toki*—at that time
消えてしまい *kiete shimai*—disappeared

まい、厚く、冷たい壁だけが残りました。

　女の子はもう一本マッチをつけました。

　すると、女の子はとても美しいクリスマスツリーの下に座っていました。

厚く *atsuku*—thick; heavy; rich
冷たい *tsumetai*—cool (to the touch)
壁だけ *kabe dake*—only the wall
残りました *nokorimashita*—left; remained
もう一本 *mō ippon*—one more (match)
つけました *tsukemashita*—lit
すると *suru to*—and then; thereupon
とても *totemo*—very
美しい *utsukushii*—beautiful
クリスマスツリー *kurisumasu tsuri*—Christmas tree
の下に *no shita ni*—under (the tree)
座っていました *suwatteimashita*—sat

そのツリーは、とても大きくて、金持ち商人の家のガラス戸を通して見たことのあるツリーよりも、もっとたくさんの飾り付けがしてありました。

何千ものロウソクの光が緑の

そのツリー *sono tsuri*—that tree
とても大きくて *totemo ookikute*—very large
金持ち *kane mochi*—rich (man)
商人 *shōnin*—merchant
の家 *no ie*—(merchant's) house
ガラス戸 *garasu do*—glass door
通して *tooshite*—through
見たことのある *mita koto no aru*—have seen
よりも *yori mo*—more than (ever seen)
もっとたくさん *motto takusan*—many more; even more
飾り付け *kazari zuke*—decorations
何千も *nansen mo*—thousands upon thousands
ロウソク *rōsoku*—candle
光 *hikari*—light
緑 *midori*—green

枝の上で燃え、店のショーウインドウの中で見たことがある色付きの絵がたくさん飾られていて、それらは女の子を見おろしていました。

少女は両手をそちらへのばしました。そのとき、マッチが消えてし

枝の上で *eda no ue de*—on the branch 文法
燃え *moe*—burning
店 *mise*—store
ショーウインドウ *sho-uindō*—show window
の中で *no naka de*—inside
見たことがある *mita koto ga aru*—have seen (in the show windows)
色付き *iro tsuki*—colored
絵 *e*—pictures
たくさん *takusan*—many
飾られていて *kazararete ite*—decorated
それら *sorera*—they (the pictures)
見おろしていました *mioroshite imashita*—looked down upon 文法
両手 *ryōte*—both hands
そちらへ *sochira e*—toward
のばしました *nobashimashita*—stretched out
そのとき *sono toki*—at that time

まいました。

クリスマスツリーの光は、どんどん女の子から離れていってしまいました。そして、女の子は今度は輝く星々を見たのです。

そのうちの一つは、長い炎の尾

クリスマスツリー *kurisumasu tsuri-*—Christmas tree
光 *hikari*—light
どんどん *dondon*—rapidly; steadily
女の子から *onna no ko kara*—from the girl
離れていってしまいました *hanarete itte shimaimashita*—separated (from girl) and left
そして *soshite*—and then
今度 *kondo*—this time
輝く *kagayaku*—shine; glitter
星々 *hoshi boshi*—stars
見た *mita*—saw
のです *no desu*—[ender showing explanations]
そのうち *sono uchi*—during that time
一つ *hitotsu*—one (glittering star)
長い炎の尾 *nagai honoo no o*—long, firey tail

を引きながら流れ落ちました。

「いま、誰かが死ぬんだわ！」
と、女の子は言いました。

女の子のおばあさん、もう死んでしまったけれど、女の子に優しくしてくれたおばあさんが、こう言っていたからです。

尾を引きながら *o wo hiki nagara*—while (falling star) leaves a trail
流れ落ちました *nagare ochimashita*—fell (the star) 文法
いま *ima*—now; just now
誰か *dare ka*—someone
死ぬん *shinun*—is dying
言いました *iimashita*—said
おばあさん *obaasan*—grandmother 文法
もう死んでしまった *mō shinde shimatta*—already passed away
けれど *keredo*—but; however
女の子に *onna no ko ni*—to the girl
優しくしてくれた *yasashiku shite kureta*—was nice (to the girl)
こう言っていた *kō itte ita*—said that
からです *kara desu*—because

星が一つ、流れ落ちるとき、魂が一つ、神さまのところへ行くのよ、と。

マッチをもう一本、壁でこすりました。すると、とても明るくなり、その光の中にはおばあさんが

星 *hoshi*—star
一つ *hitotsu*—one (star)
流れ落ちるとき *nagare ochiru toki*—when (star) falls
魂 *tamashii*—soul
神様 *kami sama*—God
ところへ *tokoro e*—to (God's) place
行くのよ *iku no yo*—goes [のよ are sentence enders indicating a confident conclusion]
と *to*—quotation marker
もう一本 *mō ippon*—one more (match)
壁で *kabe de*—on the wall
こすりました *kosurimashita*—struck (match)
すると *suruto*—upon doing so; and then
とても明るくなり *totemo akaruku nari*—became very bright
その光の中に *sono hikari no naka ni*—in that light
おばあさん *obaasan*—grandmother

立っていました。

とてもはっきりと、輝いて、優しそうで、祝福された姿で。

「おばあちゃん！」と女の子は、叫びました。

「お願い、わたしを連れてっ

立っていました *tatte imashita*—was standing
はっきりと *hakkiri to*—clearly
輝いて *kagayaite*—glittering; shining
優しそうで *yasashisō de*—with kindness; with tenderness
祝福された *shukufuku sareta*—was blessed
姿 *sugata*—figure
「おばあちゃん！」 *obaachan!*—grandma 文法
と *to*—(quotation marker)
叫びました *sakebimashita*—shouted; screamed
お願い *onegai*—please
わたし *watashi*—I; me
連れてって *tsuretette*—take (me)

て！ マッチが燃えつきたら、おばあちゃんも行ってしまう。

あったかいストーブみたいに、おいしそうなガチョウみたいに、それから、あの大きなクリスマスツリーみたいに、おばあちゃんも消えてしまう！」

少女は急いで、残ったマッチの

燃えつきたら *moe tsukitara*—if burnt out (the matches)
おばあちゃんも *obaachan mo*—grandma also
行ってしまう *itte shimau*—will leave
あったかいストーブ *attakai suto-bu*—the warm stove 文法
みたいに *mitai ni*—like (the warm stove)
おいしそうなガチョウ *oishi sō na gachō*—the delicious looking goose
それから *sore kara*—and also
あの大きな *ano ookina*—that large
消えてしまう *kiete shimau*—(will) disappear (unfortunately)
急いで *isoide*—hurriedly
残ったマッチ *nokotta macchi*—the remaining matches

束を全部壁にこすりつけました。

おばあさんを失いたくなかったのです。

マッチの束はとてもまばゆい光を放ち、昼間よりも明るくなりました。

このときほどおばあさんが美し

束 *taba*—bundle (of matches)
全部 *zenbu*—all
壁に *kabe ni*—on the wall
こすりつけました *kosuri tsukemashita*—lit; struck (the matches)
失いたくなかった *ushinaitakunakatta*—didn't want to lose (grandmother)
とてもまばゆい光 *totemo mabayui hikari*—very dazzling light
放ち *hanachi*—released; let loose (light)
昼間よりも *hiruma yori mo*—more so than in daytime
明るくなりました *akaruku narimashita*—became bright
このときほど *kono toki hodo*—like such a time as this... 文法
美しく *utsukushiku*—beautifully

く、素晴らしく見えたことはありません。

　おばあさんは、女の子をその腕の中に抱いて、高く飛んでいきました。二人は、輝く光と喜びに包まれて、やがて、もはや寒くもな

素晴らしく *subarashiku*—wonderfully; magnificently
見えたことはありません *mieta koto wa arimasen*—has never seen such a thing
おばあさん *obaasan*—grandmother
女の子 *onna no ko*—girl
その腕の中に *sono ude no naka ni*—in those arms
抱いて *daite*—hugged; held
高く飛んでいきました *takaku tonde ikimashita*—rose and flew away
文法
二人 *futari*—the two of them; two people
輝く光 *kagayaku hikari*—glittering light
喜びに *yorokobi ni*—with joy
包まれて *tsutsumarete*—wrapped (with joy)
やがて *yagate*—finally; before long
もはや *mohaya*—already; not any longer
寒くもなく *samuku mo naku*—no more cold

く、空腹もなく、恐れもないところ、神さまのみもとに行ったのです。

　しかし、次の朝、家の角には頬を赤くして、口元に笑みを浮かべて

空腹もなく *kuufuku mo naku*—no hunger
恐れもない *osore mo nai*—no fears
ところ *tokoro*—place
神様の *kamisama no*—God's...
みもとに *mimoto ni*—presence
行った *itta*—went; left
のです *no desu*—[sentence ender showing explanation]
しかし *shikashi*—but; however
次の朝 *tsugi no asa*—next morning
家の *ie no*—the house's...
角に *kado ni*—corner (of house)
頬 *hoo*—cheek (of her face)
赤くして *akaku shite*—was reddened
口元に *kuchimoto ni*—around (her) mouth
笑み *emi*—smile
浮かべて *ukabete*—floated

女の子が座っていました。

そう、一年の最後の日に、凍えて死んでいたのでした。

新年の朝の太陽は登り、女の子の体を照らしました。古いエプロンにはマッチがたくさん入っていま

座っていました *suwatte imashita*—sat; was sitting
そう *sō*—yes; that is correct
一年の *ichinen no*—one year's (last day)
最後の日に *saigo no hi ni*—on the last day
凍えて死んでいた *kogoete shinde ita*—froze to death 文法
新年の *shinnen no*—New Year's...
朝の太陽 *asa no taiyō*—morning sun
登り *nobori*—rising
体 *karada*—body
照らしました *terashimashita*—(New Year's sun) shined upon (her body)
古い *furui*—old
エプロン *epuron*—apron
たくさん *takusan*—many
入っていました *haitteimashita*—was inserted (matches in apron)

したが、一たばは燃え尽きていました。

「あったかくしようと思ったんだなあ。」と、人々は言いました。

女の子がどんなに美しいものを見たのかを知る人は、誰一人いませ

が ga—but; however
一たば hito taba—one bunch (of matches)
燃え尽きていました moe tsukite imashita—burned up completely
あったかくしよう attakaku shiyō—intending to warm (herself) 文法
と思ったん to omottan—(she) thought
だなあ da naa—[copula with sentence ender indicating emotion]
と to—[quotation marker]
人々 hito bito—people
言いました iimashita—said
女の子 onna no ko—girl
どんなに donna ni—how much; how
美しいもの utsukushii mono—a beautiful thing
見た mita—saw
のか no ka—[sentence ender often showing sorrow of what was just said]
知る人 shiru hito—person in the know (of what the girl was seeing)
誰一人 dare hitori—no one; nobody

んでした。女の子が、新しい年の喜びに満ち、おばあさんといっしょにすばらしいところへ行ったのだとは、誰も知らなかったのです。

いませんでした *imasen deshita*—wasn't there (even a person)
新しい年 *atarashii toshi*—a new year
喜び *yorokobi*—joy
に満ち *ni michi*—was full
おばあさん *obaasan*—grandmother
といっしょに *to issho ni*—together with (grandmother)
すばらしい *subarashii*—wonderful
ところへ *tokoro e*—to a (wonderful) place
行った *itta*—went
のだ *no da*—[ender showing explanation]
と *to*—[quote particle]
誰も *dare mo*—no one
知らなかった *shiranakatta*—didn't know

The Little Match Girl Grammatical Notes

1. とても寒い日のことでした *totemo samui hi no koto deshita*—it happened on a very cold day.

    とても寒い *totemo samui*—very cold; the のこと *no koto* represents an intangible thing or happening.

2. 降っていて *futte ite*—falling (snowing)

    いて is the て form of いる *iru:* to be falling; the て form connects two phrases.

3. その寒さ *sono samusa*—that degree of coldness

    The —さ shows a degree or condition: "-ness"; 高さ *taka sa*—height; how high; 難しさ *muzukashi sa*—difficultness; how difficult

4. 暗闇 *kurayami*—darkness; the dark

    Kanji makes Japanese complicated but also incredibly fascinating. These two kanji 暗闇 both have a meaning of "darkness." Together, all the more so. 暗 darkness; shade; disappear + 闇 get dark; gloomy; disorder

5. 中 *naka*—in the midst (of the darkness)

    暗闇の中 *kurayami no naka*—in the midst of darkness; 森の中 *mori no naka*—in the forest; トンネルの中 *tonneru no naka*—in the tunnel; 夢の中 *yume no naka*—in the midst of a dream

6. 歩いていました *aruite imashita*—had walked

    〜ていました *~te imashita* shows that something or someone started something (in this case, walking), and continued for a while: "-ing"; this is the past tense.

7. 何もかぶらず *nani mo kaburazu*—wasn't wearing anything

   何も means "nothing" or "not any" and requires a negative verb. The —ず makes it negative.

8. ときに *toki ni*—at the time (of leaving)

   Use with the simple verb form: 出るときに *deru toki ni*—when leaving; 食べるときに *taberu toki ni*—at the time to eat

9. 何の役にも立ちませんでした *nan no yaku ni mo tachimasen deshita*—was of no usefulness

   This phrase combines 何にも *nani ni mo* (nothing at all) with 役に立ちません *yaku ni tachimasen* (not useful); 何にも requires a negative verb.

10. 大きすぎた *ooki sugita*—was too big

    ~すぎ adds the "too much": 食べすぎ *tabe sugi*—to eat too much; 早すぎ *hayasugi*—too early/too fast; 小さすぎ *chiisasugi*—too small

11. 渡ろうとした *watarō to shita*—intended to cross (the street)

    Both 渡ろう *watarō* and とする *to suru* show intent

12. 二台 *ni dai*—two (carriages)

    台 *dai* is a counter for machines or vehicles

13. 馬車 *basha*—(a horse-drawn) carriage; coach

    Learning kanji can greatly increase your comprehension even if you haven't encountered a word before. If you knew that 馬

meant "horse" and 車 meant "car" or "vehicle," you could probably guess 馬車 means "horse drawn carriage."

14. 無くしてしまった *naku shite shimatta*—unfortunately lost (the shoes)

    しまいました shows some completion of an action often with some regret.

15. のです *no desu*—(sentence ender showing explanation or emphasis)

    This can also be shortened as んです *n desu*. "It is that…" "the fact is…" "the reason behind that is…"

16. 片方 *katahō*—one (of the shoes)

    Literally, "one side"; 片思い *kata omoi*—unrequited love (one-sided love); 片手 *kata te*—one hand

17. もう片方は *mō katahō wa*—the other one

    The もう here means more; further; other; again

18. 両足 *ryōashi*—both feet

    The 両 *ryō* means "both": 両手 *ryōte*—both hands; 両腕 *ryōude*—both arms; 両国 *ryōkoku*—both countries

19. 一たば *hito taba*—one bundle (of matches)

    たば (kanji: 束) means "bundle" or "bunch" and is used with things that can be gathered into a bunch like paper money or letters. Use *hito* instead of *ichi*.

20. 何も *nani mo*—nothing
    誰も *dare mo*—no one
    どこも *doko mo*—nowhere

    These end with a negative verb. 誰も食べなかった *dare mo tabenakatta*—No one ate.

21. 震えながら *furue nagara*—while shaking

    〜ながら means "while" or "during"; add after the ~*masu* form of a verb (but drop the actual *-masu* part): 食べながら *tabenagara*—while eating; 見ながら *mi nagara*—while watching; 勉強しながら *benkyō shinagara*—while studying

22. 舞い降りました *maiorimashita*—swoop down upon (hair)

    舞 means "dance" and 降 means "descend."

23. なんか *nanka*—things like; something like that (emphasis)

    The sentence would make sense without this word. なんか is used to emphasize the fact she wouldn't be thinking of this.

24. どの *dono*—every; any

    When taking the meaning of "every," this is followed by a も: どの人も *dono hito mo*—every person; どの道も *dono michi mo*—every road; どの場合にも *dono baai ni mo*—whichever the case may be

25. 大晦日 *oomisoka*—New Year's Eve

    Since the New Year's holiday is very important in Japan, there are special words. 晦日 *misoka* means the last day of the month. Adding 大 *oo* to it, makes it "the great last day of the month" or "New Year's Eve."

26. わ *wa*—(feminine sentence ender)

   Japanese has several gender specific markers. Except in a few dialects, わ is only used by women and it indicates emotion or admiration. A masculine ender used for asserting one's beliefs is ぞ. A feminine first person pronoun is あたし; a masculine pronoun is おれ.

27. 小さな足 *chiisa na ashi*—small legs

   足 *ashi* can mean either "leg" or "foot." Here, the match girl is pulling her legs underneath herself, but you could just as easily say she pulled her feet underneath herself.

28. 一本も *ippon mo*—not even one (match)

   本 *hon* is a counter for long, cylindrical objects. The sound changes to "*pon*" or "*bon*" after certain sounds.

29. 帰れば *kaereba*—if return (home)

   〜ば is a ender particle meaning if ... then

30. 寒いのです *samui no desu*—it's cold

   The の is for explanatory emphasis.

31. 吹き込んでくる *fuki konde kuru*—come blowing in

   吹く *fuku*—to blow + 込む *komu*—to crowd into

32. 何という *nan to iu*—how (bright)!

   何と *nanto* is often used for emphasis.

33. 温かく *atatakaku*—warming

Use 温かい *atatakai* generally and 暖かい *atatakai* when talking about the hot weather. They both mean "hot" or "warm" however.

34. のようでした *no yō deshita*—as if (it were a candle)

    よう means "similar to" or "like this." It is often interchangable with みたい: 猫のように *neko no yō ni*—like a cat

35. あたたまろうとしました *atatamarō to shimashita*—in order to warm (her legs)

    とする is a useful expression that shows intention: "to decide to…" "to suppose that…" "to intend…"

36. 燃え尽きた *moe tsukita*—burned out

    燃える *moeru* (to burn) + 尽きる *tsukiru* (to exhaust; run out of)

37. もう一本 *mō ippon*—one more (match)

    Use this construction to say one more of something: もう一回 *mō ikkai*—one more time; もう一枚 *mou ichi mai*—one more piece (of paper)

38. 豪華な *gōka na*—elegant; splendor; gorgeous

    A useful expression is 豪華絢爛 *gōkakenran*—elegant and luxurious. If someone prepares a great meal for you, say this as a compliment.

39. 刺したまま *sashita mama*—left stabbed (the knife)

    〜まま indicates a condition that doesn't change "as it is": パジャマのまま *pajama no mama*—still in pajamas; 開けたまま *aketa mama*—still open (window, door, etc)

40. 枝の上で *eda no ue de*—on the branch

    Literally, "branch's-above-on"

41. 見おろしています *mi oroshiteimasu*—look down; overlook

    見る *miru* (to see) + おろす *orosu* (to go down; to lower); this can also have the idiomatic meaning of despising someone: "to look down on someone."

42. 星々 *hoshi boshi*—stars

    The 々 symbol shows a repetition of a word. Sometimes the first sound changes as in this example. The other example in our story is 人々 *hito bito*—people

43. 流れ落ちました *nagare ochimashita*—fell (the star)

    流れる *nagareru*—to stream; to flow (liquid; time) + 落ちる *ochiru*—to fall; to drop

44. おばあさん *obaasan*—grandmother

    Be careful to not confuse おばあさん *obaasan* (grandmother; old lady) with おばさん *obasan* (aunt; ma'am).

45. 「おばあちゃん！」 *obaachan*—grandma

    The ちゃん is more familiar. [The 「」 are quotation]

46. あったかいストーブ *attakai suto-bu*—the warm stove

    This is the girl speaking in her casual speech so あたたかい *atatakai* (warm) is shortened to あったかい *attakai*.

47. このときほど *kono toki hodo*—like such a moment as this

    ほど means degree or extent. "Her grandmother had never seemed so beautiful and large as now (as the degree she is at this time)."

48. 高く飛んでいきました *takaku tonde ikimashita*—rose and flew away

    高い *takai*—high + 飛ぶ *tobu*—fly

49. 凍えて死んでいた *kogoete shinde ita*—froze to death

    凍える *kogoeru*—to freeze + 死ぬ *shinu*—to die

50. あったかくしよう *attakaku shiyō*—intending to warm (herself)

    This is in abbreviated form to show a spoken dialect.

The Little Match-Seller *in Japanese*
マッチ売りの少女

とても寒い日のことでした。雪も降っていて、もうあたりはすっかり暗くなっていて、それは今年さいごの夜のことでした。

その寒さと暗闇の中、一人のかわいそうな女の子が道を歩いていました。

頭に何もかぶらず、裸足でした。

家を出るときには確かに靴をはいていました。

でも、靴は何の役にも立ちませんでした。それは大きすぎたのです。昔、女の子のお母さんがはいていたものでした。

女の子が道を渡ろうとした時、二台の馬車がすごい速さで走ってきたので、彼女は靴を無くしてしまったのです。

片方の靴はどこにも見つかりませんでした。もう片方は、男の子が持っていってしまいました。自分に

子供ができたら、ゆりかごにするんだと言って。

それで女の子は小さな裸の足で歩いていきました。

両足は冷たさのために赤く、また青くなっていました。

女の子は、古いエプロンの中にたくさんのマッチを入れていて、手にその一たばを持っていました。

その日一日、誰も女の子から何も買ってくれませんでした。

一円だってくれる人はいなかっ

たのです。

寒さと空腹で震えながら、女の子は歩き回りました。かわいそうな子、まさに悲惨を絵に描いたようです。

雪が少女の長い金髪に舞い降りました。

その髪は首のまわりに美しくカールして下がっています。

でも、もちろん、女の子は美しさのことなんか考えていません。

どの窓からも明かりが輝き、通

りには ガチョウを焼いているおいしそうな香りがしました。

「今日は大晦日だわ。」女の子はそう思いました。

二つの家が街の角に並んで立っていました。

そのうち片方が前にせり出しています。

女の子はそこに座って小さくなりました。女の子は小さな足を体の下に引き寄せましたが、女の子はどんどん寒くなってきました。

けれど、家に帰るなんてできませんでした。

マッチは一本も売れていないし、たったの一円ももらえなかったのですから、このまま帰ればお父さんに殴られてしまいます。

それに家だって寒いのです。

頭の上に天井はありましたが、ビュービューと風が吹き込んでくるのです。わらとボロ布で塞いではありますが、大きなひびが入っているからです。

女の子の小さな両手は冷たさの

ためにもう何も感じなくなっていました。

　ああ！マッチがあるわ。たばの中からマッチを取り出して、壁にこすり付けて、火をつければ指を温められるわ。

　女の子は、マッチを一本取り出しました。　シュッ！　何という輝き。何とよく燃えることでしょう。

　温かく、輝く炎で、上に手をかざすとまるで小さなロウソクのようでした。

すばらしい光です。女の子はまるで大きな鉄のストーブの前に座っているように思いました。

そのストーブには光るしんちゅうの足があり、上にはしんちゅうの飾りがついていました。

なんと美しく燃える炎でしょう。

炎はまわりをあたためます。

女の子は足をのばして、あたたまろうとしました。

しかし、——小さな炎は消

え、ストーブも消えてしまいました。

手の中に燃え尽きたマッチだけが残っているだけでした。

女の子はもう一本壁にこすりました。マッチは明るく燃え、その明かりが壁にあたったところはヴェールのように透けて見えました。そして、女の子にはその向こうに部屋が見えました。

テーブルの上にはとても白いテーブルクロスが広げられ、その上には豪華な食器が並べられていまし

た。

　焼かれたガチョウにはりんごとプラムが詰められていて、おいしそうな湯気を上げていました。

　そして、うれしいことに、ガチョウは、背中にナイフとフォークを刺したまま、テーブルから飛び降りて、よろよろと歩きながら、かわいそうな女の子のところまでやってきたのです。

　と、その時、マッチは消えてしまい、厚く、冷たい壁だけが残りました。

女の子はもう一本マッチをつけました。

すると、女の子はとても美しいクリスマスツリーの下に座っていました。

そのツリーは、とても大きくて、金持ち商人の家のガラス戸を通して見たことのあるツリーよりも、もっとたくさんの飾り付けがしてありました。

何千ものロウソクの光が緑の枝の上で燃え、店のショーウインドウの中で見たことがある色付きの

絵がたくさん飾られていて、それらは女の子を見おろしていました。

少女は両手をそちらへのばしました。そのとき、マッチが消えてしまいました。

クリスマスツリーの光は、どんどん女の子から離れていってしまいました。そして、女の子は今度は輝く星々を見たのです。

そのうちの一つは、長い炎の尾を引きながら流れ落ちました。

「いま、誰かが死ぬんだわ！」

と、女の子は言いました。

女の子のおばあさん、もう死んでしまったけれど、女の子に優しくしてくれたおばあさんが、こう言っていたからです。

星が一つ、流れ落ちるとき、魂が一つ、神さまのところへ行くのよ、と。

マッチをもう一本、壁でこすりました。すると、とても明るくなり、その光の中にはおばあさんが立っていました。

とてもはっきりと、輝いて、優

しそうで、祝福された姿で。

「おばあちゃん！」と女の子は、叫びました。

「お願い、わたしを連れてって！マッチが燃えつきたら、おばあちゃんも行ってしまう。

あったかいストーブみたいに、おいしそうなガチョウみたいに、それから、あの大きなクリスマスツリーみたいに、おばあちゃんも消えてしまう！」

少女は急いで、残ったマッチの束を全部壁にこすりつけました。

おばあさんを失いたくなかったのです。

　マッチの束はとてもまばゆい光を放ち、昼間よりも明るくなりました。

　このときほどおばあさんが美しく、素晴らしく見えたことはありません。

　おばあさんは、女の子をその腕の中に抱いて、高く飛んでいきました。二人は、輝く光と喜びに包まれて、やがて、もはや寒くもなく、空腹もなく、恐れもないとこ

ろ、神さまのみもとに行ったのです。

しかし、次の朝、家の角には頬を赤くして、口元に笑みを浮かべて女の子が座っていました。

そう、一年の最後の日に、凍えて死んでいたのでした。

新年の朝の太陽は登り、女の子の体を照らしました。古いエプロンにはマッチがたくさん入っていましたが、一束は燃え尽きていました。

「あったかくしようと思ったん

だなあ。」と、人々は言いました。

女の子がどんなに美しいものを見たのかを知る人は、誰一人いませんでした。女の子が、新しい年の喜びに満ち、おばあさんといっしょにすばらしいところへ行ったのだとは、誰も知らなかったのです。

The Little Match Girl English Summary
Please try to tackle the Japanese first and use this only as needed.

This is the 1913 translation by H.L. Brækstad

IT was terribly cold; the snow was falling, and the dark evening was setting in; it was the last evening of the year—New Year's Eve.

In this cold and uncomfortable darkness, a poor little girl, bareheaded and barefooted, was walking through the streets. She had certainly had some sort of slippers on when she left her home, but they were not of much use to her, as they were very large slippers. Her mother had used them last, so you can guess they were large ones.

As the little girl ran across the street just as two carriages were passing at a terrible rate, she lost the slippers. One of the slippers could not be found, and the other a boy ran away with. He said he would use it for a cradle when he got children of his own.

There was the little girl walking about on her naked little feet; they were red and blue with cold. In an old pinafore she had some bundles of matches, and in her hand she carried one of them.

No one had bought anything of her the whole day, and no one had given her a penny. Hungry and shivering, she passed on, poor little girl, looking the very picture of misery.

The snowflakes fell on her long yellow hair, which curled itself so beautifully about her neck; but of course she had no thoughts for such vanities. Lights were shining in all the windows, and there was such a delicious smell of roast goose in the street. "Ah! it is New Year's Eve," she thought.

Over in a corner between two houses—the one projected a little beyond the other—she crouched down, with her little feet drawn up under her; but she felt colder and colder, and she dared not go home, for she had not sold any matches or got a single penny; her father would beat her, and, besides, it was just as cold at home. They certainly had a roof over their heads, but through this the wind whistled, although they had stopped the largest cracks with rags and straw.

Her little hands were quite benumbed with cold. Ah! a match might do some good. If she only dared to take one out of the bundle and rub it against the wall, and warm her fingers over the flame! She took one out—ratch!—how it spurted, how it burned! It was a warm, clear flame, just like a little candle, when she held her hand round it. It was a wonderful light; the little girl thought she was sitting right before a great iron stove with bright brass feet and brass mountings. How beautiful the fire burned! How it warmed her! But what was that? The little girl stretched her feet out to warm them also, and the flame went out—the stove vanished—she had only the small stump of the burned match in her hand.

A new match was rubbed against the wall; it burned, it gave a beautiful light, and where the light fell on the wall it became transparent like a veil. She could see right into the room, where the table was covered with a bright white cloth, and on it a fine china dinner service; the roast goose, stuffed with prunes and apples, was steaming beautifully. But, what was still more delightful, the goose jumped from the dish and waddled along the floor, with knife and fork in its back, straight toward the poor girl. When the match went out, there was only the thick, cold wall to be seen.

She lighted a new match. Then she was sitting under a beautiful Christmas-tree; it was still larger and more decorated than that she had seen through the glass door at the rich merchant's last Christmas. Thousands of candles burned upon the green branches, and colored pictures, like those that you see in the shop windows, were looking down upon her. The little girl stretched both her hands toward them—and the match went out. The light seemed to go farther and farther away from her. She saw now that they were the bright stars. One of them fell down, leaving a long train of fire after it.

"Now some one is dying," said the little one. Her old grandmother, who was the only one who had been good to her, but was now dead, had told her when a star falls a soul goes to God.

She rubbed a match again on the wall. It gave such a light, and in its luster stood the old grandmother—so clear, so bright, so mild, so blessed!

"Grandmother," cried the little one, "oh, take me with you! I know you will be gone when the match goes out—gone, just like the warm stove, the beautiful roast goose, and the great, beautiful Christmas tree." And she rubbed quickly all the remaining matches in the bundle,—she would not lose her grandmother,—and the matches burned with such a splendor that it was brighter than in the middle of the day. Grandmother had never before been so beautiful, so grand. She took the little girl in her arms, and they flew away in brightness and joy, so high—high, where there was no cold, no hunger, no fear—they were with God!

But, next morning, in the corner by the house sat the little girl with red cheeks and a smile about her mouth, dead—frozen to death on the last evening of the old year. The sun of New Year's morning rose up on the little corpse, with the matches in the pinafore, and one bundle nearly burned. "She wanted to warm herself," said the people. No one knew what beautiful visions she had had, and in what splendor she had gone into the New Year's joy and happiness with her old grandmother.

Kanji in Focus

The following are a few of the most important kanji found in this book. The underlined reading is probably the most used. If there is a . that means what comes before the dot is in the kanji and what goes after the dot follows the kanji in hiragana.

寒
- READINGS: カン; <u>さむ.い</u>
- MEANING: cold
- EXAMPLE: 寒中水泳 (かんちゅうすいえい) swimming in the middle of winter

降
- READINGS: コウ; ゴ; お.りる; <u>ふ.る</u>
- MEANING: descend; fall (rain or snow)
- EXAMPLE: 降雪 (こうせつ) snowfall

暗
- READINGS: アン; <u>くら.い</u>; くら.む; くれ.る
- MEANING: darkness; disappear; shade
- EXAMPLE: 暗殺 (あんさつ) assassination

夜
- READINGS: ヤ; よ; <u>よる</u>
- MEANING: night; evening
- EXAMPLE: 夜中 (よなか) midnight; middle of the night

髪
- READINGS: ハツ; <u>かみ</u>
- MEANING: hair (on head)
- EXAMPLE: 散髪 (さんぱつ) hair-cutting

空
- **READINGS:** クウ; そら; あ.く; から
- **MEANING:** empty; sky; void
- **EXAMPLE:** 空手(からて) karate

飾
- **READINGS:** ショク; かざ.る; かざ.り
- **MEANING:** decorate; ornament; adorn; embellish
- **EXAMPLE:** 飾(かざ)りのテープ decorative tape

輝
- **READINGS:** キ; かがや.く
- **MEANING:** radiance; shine; sparkle
- **EXAMPLE:** 輝(かがや)く星(ほし) glittering star

雪
- **READINGS:** セツ; ゆき
- **MEANING:** snow
- **EXAMPLE:** 大雪(おおゆき) heavy snow

道
- **READINGS:** ドウ; トウ; みち
- **MEANING:** road; street; course; teachings
- **EXAMPLE:** 近道(ちかみち) short cut

腹
- **READINGS:** フク; はら
- **MEANING:** abdomen; belly; stomach
- **EXAMPLE:** 空腹(くうふく) hunger

歩
- **READINGS**: ホ; ブ; フ; <u>ある.く</u>; あゆ.む
- **MEANING**: walk; counter for steps
- **EXAMPLE**: 散歩(さんぽ) walk; stroll

頭
- **READINGS**: トウ; ズ; <u>あたま</u>; かしら
- **MEANING**: head; counter for large animals
- **EXAMPLE**: 頭金(あたまきん) down payment; deposit

何
- **READINGS**: カ; <u>なに</u>; なん
- **MEANING**: what
- **EXAMPLE**: 幾何学(きかがく) geometry

足
- **READINGS**: ソク; <u>あし</u>; た.りる; た.す
- **MEANING**: leg; foot; be sufficient
- **EXAMPLE**: 足跡(あしあと) footprints

家
- **READINGS**: カ; ケ; <u>いえ</u>; や; うち
- **MEANING**: house; home; family; expert
- **EXAMPLE**: 家庭(かてい) household

片
- **READINGS**: ヘン; <u>かた</u>
- **MEANING**: one-sided; sheet
- **EXAMPLE**: 片道(かたみち) one-way trip

方

READINGS: ホウ; <u>かた</u>
MEANING: direction; person; alternative
EXAMPLE: 考(かんが)え方(かた) way of thinking

靴

READINGS: カ; <u>くつ</u>
MEANING: shoes
EXAMPLE: 靴(くつ)下 socks; stockings

壁

READINGS: へき; <u>かべ</u>
MEANING: wall; fence
EXAMPLE: 壁(かべ)紙(がみ) wallpaper

炎

READINGS: エン; ほのお
MEANING: inflammation; flame; blaze
EXAMPLE: 嫉(しっ)妬(と)の炎(ほのお) flames of jealousy

燃

READINGS: ネン; も.える; も.やす; も.す
MEANING: burn; blaze; glow
EXAMPLE: 化(か)石(せき)燃(ねん)料(りょう) fossil fuel

VOCABULARY

「」 quotation marks

A

ああ！ aa!–ah!

あたたまろうとしました atatamarō to shimashita–intending to warm (her legs)

あたためます atatamemasu– to warm

あたった atatta–hit; touched (where the light fell)

あたり atari–the area; nearby

あったかいストーブ attakai suto-bu–the warm stove

あったかくしよう attakaku shiyō–intending to warm (herself)

あの大きな ano ookina–that large

あり ari–have

ありますが arimasu ga–existed, but...

上げていました agete imashita–raised; elevated

厚く atsuku–thick; heavy; rich

明かり akari–light; illumination

明るくなりました akaruku narimashita–became bright

明るく燃え akaruku moe–burned brightly

新しい年 atarashii toshi–a new year

朝の太陽 asa no taiyō–morning sun

歩いていました aruite imashita–had walked

歩きながら aruki nagara–while walking

歩き回りました aruki mawarimashita–walked around

温かく atatakaku–warming

温められる atatamerareru–be able to warm (fingers)

赤く akaku–(turned) red

赤くして akaku shite–was reddened

頭に atama ni–on (her) head (the に indicates location)

頭の上に atama no ue ni–above (one's) head

青く aoku–(turned) blue

足をのばして ashi o nobashite–stretch out (her) legs

B

ビュービューと byu- byu- to–whistling (sound)

ボロぬの boro nuno–worn out cloth

馬車 basha–horse drawn carriage; coach

C

小さくなりました chiisaku narimashita–became small

小さな chiisa na–small

小さな両手 chiisa na ryōte–both small hands

小さな炎 chiisa na honoo–a small flame

小さな足 chiisa na ashi–small legs

D

だけ dake–only

だって datte–after all; because

だなあ da naa–(copula with sentence ender indicating emotion)

できたら dekitara–if (he has children)

できませんでした dekimasen deshite–couldn't (return home)

でしょう deshō–I think

でも demo–but; however

どこにも doko ni mo–nowhere (use with negative verb)

どの dono–every; any

どの窓からも dono mado kara mo–from any window

どんどん don don–rapidly; steadily

どんなに donna ni–how much; how

出るときに deru toki ni–at the time of leaving

抱いて daite–hugged; held

誰か dare ka–someone

誰も dare mo–no one

誰一人 dare hitori–no one; nobody

E

エプロン epuron–apron

笑み emi–smile

絵 e–picture; painting

枝の上で eda no ue de–on the branch

F

フォーク fo-ku–fork

二つの futatsu no–two (houses)

二人 futari–the two of them; two people

古い furui–old

吹き込んでくる fuki konde kuru–come blowing in

塞いで fusaide–closed; blocked; shut up

降っていて futte ite–falling (snowing)

震えながら furue nagara–while shaking

G

が ga–but; however

ガラス戸 garasu do–glass door

鵞鳥 gachō–goose

豪華 gōka–gorgeous; splendor

H

はいていました haite imashita–was wearing (shoes)

はっきりと hakkiri to–clearly

ひび hibi–crack

一たば hito taba–one bunch (of matches)

一つ hitotsu–one (star)

一人 hitori–one person

人 hito–person

人々 hito bito–people

光 hikari–light

光る真鍮 hikaru shinchuu–shining brass

入っていました haitteimashita–was inserted (matches in apron)

入っている haitte iru–entered; opened up (cracks)

星 hoshi–star

星々 hoshi boshi–stars

放ち hanachi–released; let loose (light)

引き寄せました hiki yosemashita–pulled toward oneself

広げられ hirogerare–spread; extend; enlarge

昼間よりも hiruma yori mo–more so than in daytime

悲惨 hisan–tragedy; misery

離れていってしまいました hanarete itte shimaimashita–separated (from girl) and left

部屋 heya–room

走ってきた hashitte kita–running (the きた is used to show

becoming, coming to be, growing)

裸のあし hadaka no ashi—naked feet; barefoot

裸足 hadashi—barefoot

火 hi—fire

炎で honoo de—with a flame

頬 hoo—cheek (of her face)

I

いなかった inakatta—weren't (any buyers)

いま ima—now; just now

いませんでした imasen deshita—wasn't there (even a person)

一円も ichien mo—even one yen

一年の ichinen no—one year's (last day)

一日 ichi nichi—all day

一本 ippon—one (match)

一本も ippon mo—not even one (match)

入れていて irete ite—were put; placed (inside)

家 ie—house

家に帰る ie ni kaeru—to return home

家の ie no–the house's...

急いで isoide–hurriedly

色付き iro tsuki–colored

行くのよ iku no yo–goes (のよ are sentence enders indicating a confident conclusion)

行った itta–went; left

行ってしまう itte shimau–will leave

言いました iimashita–said

言って itte–saying

1円 ichi en–one yen

J

自分に jibun ni–to himself (have children himself)

K

かざす kazasu–to hold up over one's head

かぶらず kaburazu–didn't wear

から kara–from

からです kara desu–because

かわいそうな kawai sō na–pitiful

かわいそうな子 kawai sō na ko–pitiful girl

くれる kureru–receive (money)

けれど keredo–but; however

こう言っていた kō itte ita–said that

こすりつけました kosuri tsukemashita–lit; struck (the matches)

こすりました kosurimashita–struck (match)

こすり付けて kosuri tsukete–strike

このときほど kono toki hodo–like such a time as this…

このまま kono mama–as is; without change

カール ka-ru–curl

クリスマスツリー kurisumasu tsuri-–Christmas tree

今年 kotoshi–this year

今年さいごの夜のことでした kotoshi saigo no yoru no koto deshita–It was the last night of the year

今度 kondo–this time

今日 kyō–today

体 karada–body

体の下に karada no shita ni–(pulled legs) under her body

凍えて死んでいた kogoete shinde ita–froze to death

壁だけ kabe dake—only the wall

壁で kabe de—on the wall

口元に kuchimoto ni—around (her) mouth

子供 kodomo—children

描いたよう kaitayō—as if drawn/painted

感じなくなっていました kanjinaku natte imashita—lost feeling

帰れば kaereba—if return (home)

暗くなっていて kuraku natte ite—it became completely dark

暗闇 kurayami—darkness

彼女 kanojo—she

風 kaze—wind

飾られていて kazararete ite—decorated

飾り付け kazari zuke—decorations

首 kubi—neck

靴 kutsu—shoe

金持ち kane mochi—rich (man)

金髪 kinpatsu—golden hair; blonde

輝いて kagayaite—glittering; shining

輝き kagayaki–bright; radiant

輝く kagayaku–shining; glittering

輝く光 kagayaku hikari–glittering light

買ってくれません katte kuremasen–wouldn't buy

考えていません kangaete imasen–didn't think of

神様 kami sama–God

神様の kamisama no–God's...

空腹で kuufuku de–with hunger

空腹もなく kuufuku mo naku–no hunger

消え kie–extinguish

消えてしまい kiete shimai–disappeared

消えてしまう kiete shimau–(will) disappear (unfortunately)

香りがしました kaori ga shimashita–had a good scent

角に kado ni–corner (of house)

片方 katahō–one side

M

まさに masa ni–certainly; truly

また mata–and; also

まで made–until

まるで marude–as if; just like

まわり mawari–around

まわりに mawari ni–around (the neck)

みたいに mitai ni–like (the warm stove)

みもとに mimoto ni–presence

もう mō–already

もう一本 mō ippon–one more (match)

もう死んでしまった mō shinde shimatta–already passed away

もう片方 mō katahō–the other side (shoe)

もちろん mochiron–of course

もっとたくさん motto takusan–many more; even more

もの mono–(used to express emotional involvement)

もはや mohaya–already; not any longer

もらえなかった moraenakatta–didn't receive

マッチ macchi–matches

前に mae ni–in front of

向こうに mukō ni–other side; opposite side

持っていました motte imashita–carried

持って行って motte itte–to take; carry (something) away

店 mise–store

昔 mukashi–a long time ago

道 michi–road; street

見えたことはありません mieta koto wa arimasen–has never seen such a thing

見えました miemashita–able to be seen

見おろしていました mioroshite imashita–looked down upon

見た mita–saw

見たことのある mita koto no aru–have seen

見つかりません mitsukarimasen–cannot be found

舞い降りました mai orimashita–swoop down upon (hair)

緑 midori–green

燃え moe–burning

燃えつきたら moe tsukitara–if burnt out (the matches)

燃える炎 moeru honoo–burning fire

燃え尽きた moe tsukita–to burn out

燃え尽きていました moe tsukite imashita–burned up completely

窓 mado–window

街の角に machi no kado ni—on a street corner

N

なっていました natte imashita—turned (blue); becoming

なんか nanka—such a thing; or something like that…

なんて nante—such as; (things) like (used for emphasis of the absurdity of something)

なんと美しく nanto utsukushiku—how beautifully (it burned)

にする ni suru—to make (shoe) into (cradle)

に殴られてしまいます ni nagurarete shimaimasu—will be hit (by father)

に満ち ni michi—was full

のか no ka—(sentence ender often showing sorrow of what was just said)

のために no tame ni—because of; due to…

のだ no da—(ender showing explanation)

のです no desu—(ender for explanations)

のばしました nobashimashita—stretched out

のようでした no yō deshita—as if (it were a candle)

のように no yō ni—like; similar to (a veil)

の下に no shita ni—under (the tree)

の中で no naka de-inside

の中に no naka ni-inside; in the midst (of the apron)

の前に no mae ni-before; in front of

の家 no ie-(merchant's) house

んだ n da-the expectation is that... (sentence ender when explaining)

ナイフ naifu-knife

並べられていました naraberarete imashita-was lined up

並んで narande-lined up

残ったマッチ nokotta macchi-the remaining matches

残っている nokotteiru-left over; remaining

残りました nokorimashita-left; remained

流れ落ちました nagare ochimashita-fell (the star)

流れ落ちるとき nagare ochiru toki-when (star) falls

長い nagai-long

長い炎の尾 nagai honoo no o-long, firey tail

2台 ni dai-two (carriages)

〜の中 ~no naka-in the midst (of the cold and darkness)

登り nobori-rising

無くしてしまった naku shite shimatta–unfortunately lost (her shoes)

O

を o–(direct object marker)

「おばあちゃん！」 obaachan!–grandma

おいしそう oishi sō–looks/smells delicious

おいしそうな鵞鳥 oishi sō na gachō–the delicious looking goose

おばあさん obaasan–grandmother

おばあちゃんも obaachan mo–grandma also

お母さん okaasan–mother

お父さん otōsan–father

お願い onegai–please

大きすぎた ooki sugita–was too big

大きな ooki na–big; large

大晦日 oomisoka–New Year's Eve

女の子 onna no ko–girl

女の子から onna no ko kara–from the girl

女の子に onna no ko ni–to the girl

尾を引きながら o wo hiki nagara—while (falling star) leaves a trail

恐れもない osore mo nai—no fears

思いました omoimashita—thought

男の子 otoko no ko—boy

P

プラム puramu—plum

R

りんご ringo—apple

ロウソク rōsoku—candle

両手 ryōte—both hands

両足 ryō ashi—both feet

蝋燭 rōsoku—candle

S

さいご saigo—last; final

し shi—(conjunction at the end of phrases that notes one of several reasons)

しかし shikashi—but; however

しまいました shimaimashita–(shows completion often with regret)

すごい速さ sugoi hayasa–very fast; extreme speed

すっかり sukkari–completely; thoroughly

すばらしい subarashii–wonderful

すばらしい光 subarashii hikari–wonderful light

すると suruto–upon doing so; and then

せり出しています seri dashite imasu–push out; to jut out; protrude

そう sō–yes; that is correct

そう思いました sō omoimashita–thought like that

そこに soko ni–there

そして soshite–and then

そちらへ sochira e–toward

その sono–that

そのうち sono uchi–during that time

そのとき sono toki–at that time

そのストーブ sono suto-bu–that stove

そのツリー sono tsuri–that tree

その一たば sono hito taba–that single bundle

その上に sono ue ni-on top of

その光の中に sono hikari no naka ni-in that light

その寒さ sono samusa-that degree of coldness

その日 sono hi-that day

その時 sono toki-at that time

その腕の中に sono ude no naka ni-in those arms

その髪 sono kami-that hair

それから sore kara-and also

それで sore de-and; thereupon; because of that

それに sore ni-besides; moreover

それは sore wa-that is; as for that…

それら sorera-they (the pictures)

シュッ！ shuu!-(effect of striking a match)

ショーウインドウ sho-uindō-show window

ストーブ suto-bu-stove

下がっています sagatte imasu-hang down (hair)

刺したまま sashita mama-left stabbed (the knife)

叫びました sakebimashita-shouted; screamed

商人 shōnin-merchant

姿 sugata–figure

寒いのです samui no desu–it's cold

寒くなってきました samuku natte kimashita–became cold

寒くもなく samuku mo naku–no more cold

寒さ samusa–degree of cold; coldness

少女 shōjo–little girl

座って suwatte–sitting

座っていました suwatte imashita–sat; was sitting

座っているように suwatte iru yō ni–as if sitting (in front of the stove)

食器 shokki–tableware

透けて sukete–transparent

背中に senaka ni–in the back

素晴らしく subarashiku–wonderfully; magnificently

祝福された shukufuku sareta–was blessed

白いテーブルクロス shiroi te-buru kurosu–white tablecloth

真鍮の足 shinchuu no ashi–brass legs (of the stove)

真鍮の飾り shinchuu no kazari–brass decorations

知らなかった shiranakatta–didn't know

知る人 shiru hito—person in the know (of what the girl was seeing)

死ぬん shinun—is dying

最後の日に saigo no hi ni—on the last day

新年の shinnen no—New Year's...

T

たくさん takusan—many

たったの tatta no—only; merely; but; no more than

たばの中から taba no naka kara—from the bundle (of matches)

ついていました tsuite imashita—were attached

つけました tsukemashita—lit

つければ tsukereba—if lit (the match)

と to—(quotation marker)

と to—and

といっしょに to issho ni—together with (grandmother)

ところ tokoro—place

ところへ tokoro e—to a place

とても totemo—very

とてもまばゆい光 totemo mabayui hikari—very dazzling light

とても大きくて totemo ookikute–very large

とても寒い totemo samui–very cold

とても寒い日のことでした totemo samui hi no koto deshita–it happened on a very cold day

とても明るくなり totemo akaruku nari–became very bright

と思ったん to omottan–(she) thought

テーブル te-buru–table

テーブルの上に te-buru no ue ni–on top of the table

冷たい tsumetai–cool (to the touch)

冷たさ tsumeta sa–coldness; the degree of cold

包まれて tsutsumarete–wrapped (with joy)

取り出して tori dashite–brought out

取り出しました tori dashimashita–brought out

天井 tenjō–ceiling

束 taba–bundle (of matches)

手 te–hand

手に te ni–in hand

手の中に te no naka ni–in (her) hands

飛び降りて tobi orite–jump down

鉄の tetsu no–an iron (stove)

通して tooshite–through

通りには toori ni wa–and on the street

連れてって tsuretette–take (me)

詰められていて tsumerarete ite–stuffed into; jammed in

立っていました tatte imashita–standing; built

確かに tashika ni–certainly; surely

次の朝 tsugi no asa–next morning

時 toki–the time (she tried to cross the street)

照らしました terashimashita–(New Year's sun) shined upon (her body)

高く飛んでいきました takaku tonde ikimashita–rose and flew away

魂 tamashii–soul

U

うれしいこと ureshii koto–a good thing; happily

上に ue ni–above

売れていない urete inai–didn't sell

失いたくなかった ushinaitakunakatta–didn't want to lose

(grandmother)

美しい utsukushii–beautiful

美しいもの utsukushii mono–a beautiful thing

美しく utsukushiku–beautifully

美しさのこと utsukushi sa no koto–(her) beautifulness

浮かべて ukabete–floated

V

ヴェール ve-ru–veil

W

わ wa–(sentence ender used by women)

わたし watashi–I; me

わらと wara to–with straw

渡ろうとした watarō to shita–intended to cross (the street)

Y

やがて yagate–finally; before long

やってきた yatte kita–came along

ゆりかご yurikago—cradle

よく燃えること yoku moeru koto—burning well

よりも yori mo—more than (ever seen)

よろよろと yoroyoro to—tottering; unsteady on its feet

優しくしてくれた yasashiku shite kureta—was nice (to the girl)

優しそうで yasashisō de—with kindness; with tenderness

喜び yorokobi—joy

喜びに yorokobi ni—with joy

夜 yoru—night

指 yubi—finger

役にも立ちませんでした yaku ni mo tachimasen deshita—not at all useful

雪 yuki—snow

雪も yuki mo—snow also (was falling)

焼いている yaite iru—cooking; frying

焼かれた yakareta—cooked

湯気 yuge—steam; vapor

Z

全部 zenbu—all

DOWNLOAD LINK

Please go to this website to download the MP3s for both stories: (There is an exclusive *free* **gift on kanji** waiting there too.)

http://japanesereaders.com/1054

Thank you for purchasing and reading this book! To contact the authors, please email them at help@thejapanshop.com. See also the wide selection of materials for learning Japanese at www.TheJapanShop.com and the free site for learning Japanese at www.TheJapanesePage.com.

www.TheJapanShop.com

Also by Clay & Yumi Boutwell

Japanese Readers Collection: Volumes 1-6

Volume 1: Hikoichi
Volume 2: Momotaro
Volume 3: Inch-high Samurai
Volume 4: The Mouse Bride
Volume 5: The Cut-Tongue Sparrow
Volume 6: Yuki Onna

Other Japanese Lesson Titles:

Japanese Grammar 100 in Plain English
101 Common Japanese Idioms in Plain English
200 More Japanese Idioms
Japanese Sentences: Haiku
Japanese Dialogues: Meeting and Greetings
Learn Japanese through Dialogues: at the Restaurant
Japanese Dialogues: Directions
Kotowaza, Japanese Proverbs and Sayings
Hiragana, the Basics of Japanese
Katakana, the Basics of Japanese
Sound Words in Japanese
Ninja Penguin Talks Japanese in Japan
100 Useful Kanji (Get it FREE at www.TheJapanShop.com)

Clay's Fiction

THE TEMPORAL SERIES
The Temporal (Get it FREE at www.ClayBoutwell.com)
A Temporal Trust

THE AGORA MYSTERIES
Two Tocks before Midnight (Get it FREE at www.ClayBoutwell.com)
The Penitent Thief
The Peace Party Massacre
The Curse of the Mad Sheik
The Captain's Play

TANAKA
Tanaka and the Yakuza's Daughter

Visit **www.ClayBoutwell.com** **for the latest information.**

Printed in Great Britain
by Amazon